"ONE LOVE is simple, clear, biblical and full of wisdom. If I still had teenagers, I would put it in their hands and make sure they read it. Some of the stories will break your heart as they did mine. Others will give evidence of the amazing grace of God and the healing power of the gospel."

Daniel L. Akin, President,
Southeastern Baptist Theological Seminary,
Wake Forest, NC

"Dale Elwell writes passionately and convincingly on the subject of sexual relationships. He uses a fresh and creative approach as he communicates the timeless truths of God's Word. This book is more than just a great read - it is a great experience when practiced!"

David Horton, President,
Fruitland Baptist Bible College, Hendersonville, NC

"This is a challenging book for challenging times. It calls us back to the people we really are."

Taylor Field, Senior Pastor,
Graffiti Church, New York City, NY

"My only regret is that I did not take advantage of the ONE LOVE conference years ago! Our youth group has participated in a couple of different programs emphasizing abstinence and sexual purity, and one of these proved to have a tangible impact on our group. However, if I had to choose only one then our youth group would be exposed to a ONE LOVE conference annually. Aside from the benefit of being delivered in person, ONE LOVE has a comprehensive approach and equips students to build a solid foundation on which to build their purity. ONE LOVE takes time to address topics that other curricula do not, and it charges head on in answering the difficult questions that teens have regarding sexuality."

Andy Cockrell, Associate Pastor,
Kenly Missionary Baptist Church, Kenly, NC

ONE LOVE
EXTREME EXPERIENCE

ONE LOVE

EXTREME
EXPERIENCE

DALE ELWELL

ONE LOVE: Extreme Experience
Published by: Cross Culture Publishing
PO BOX 4144
Greensboro, NC 27404 U.S.A.

ISBN-13: 978-0692235126
ISBN-10: 0692235124

Cover & Interior Design: Brooke Horn
Book images and illustrations by: Brooke Horn
Author photo: Crystal Faulkiner, 2014

The testimonies in this book are actual, however, some of the names have been changed at the individuals' request.

Printed in the United States of America
First Edition 2014

TO THE FATHER

"May they be in us, just as you are in me and I am in you....I in them and you in me, so that they may be completely one, in order that the world may know that you sent me and that you love them as you love me."

--Jesus
John 17:20-23 GNT

TO MY PARENTS:
Rev. D.D. and June Elwell—

Dad, you demonstrated undying love and showed your children how a man should treat a woman. You honored and cherished your bride for 61 ½ years. Christ's love for His bride is the legacy you gave us. May all your children, grandchildren, & great grandchildren let that legacy shine in our own marriages!

Mom, you are not only an amazing woman of God, but an incredible testimony of loyalty to the husband of your youth. The strength that so many saw in Dad was largely a reflection of the support you gave him. You showed me what kind of woman I should look for in a bride. By God's grace, I found her! Thank you.

TO MY WIFE:
Brantlee, you are my beloved bride.
Through you, God has made my
"one love" experience extremely awesome!

TO OUR CHILDREN:
Caleb, Andrew, Hannah, & Hope,
I pray that God engrain these principles into your hearts
and grant you a "one love" experience that is
extremely AWESOME!

CONTENTS

FOREWORD

Dale Elwell is a godly husband and father, a student of culture, an evangelist, a youth speaker, a conference leader, a writer, and he is my friend. Dale has a great heart to see our culture changed towards authentic biblical Christianity. Dale does conferences and retreats to help young people understand what biblical, God-honoring, true "one love" is all about. This book is a collection of the great truths that he shares.

In this book, *ONE LOVE*, Dale focuses on the "why" and not just on the "what" and "how" of a godly relationship. He carefully and consistently reminds us that without a personal relationship with God through Jesus Christ it will be a great challenge to have a good and godly marriage relationship with one another as well as a potentially disastrous dating relationship. Dale includes an explanation on how to have a personal relationship with Jesus Christ. Every Christian book needs this careful explanation of the Gospel. Thank you Dale!

ONE LOVE is a great tool for youth and college students to read and for youth pastors to use to train and prepare young people to focus on the right things in order to have healthy relationships! It is also a great tool for parents to use to prepare their children to experience fulfillment in marriage and a positive sexual relationship.

Youth pastors should purchase this book by the masses and distribute it to their parents to give to their children as a gift or at the least a stocking stuffer at Christmas! Every young person needs to be taught these Biblical principals on healthy sexual relationships—the younger the better!

Church leaders have shied away from this topic too often and for way too long. Dale gives very simple and practical Biblical concepts and spiritual foundations for a God-honoring sexual relationship.

The "Process of Sex" is a very important chapter to be read and to explain to anyone and everyone who enters a dating relationship. Getting the "process" right will lead to a more fulfilling relationship.

ONE LOVE has great reminders for fathers on the role and responsibility we have to protect and prepare our daughters as well as how to train young men who may come calling as to the expectations and responsibility that is transferred to them when dating or courting our daughters.

The message on "courtship" is excellent and needs to be read and understood by everyone. Dale shares both the tragic reality of our morally indifferent culture contrasted against the ideals of courtship. One Love also compares the differences and benefits of courtship versus modern "dating."

I thank Dale Elwell for writing this much needed book and I fully recommend this book to you and Dale as a speaker and conference leader that you should have in your church or conference!

--Marty Dupree,
Senior Consultant of Evangelism and Discipleship,
Baptist State Convention of North Carolina

INTRODUCTION

In order to have dreadlocks, a person must allow several strands of hair to bond together. This is pretty cool...as long as the person wants to keep the dreadlocks. The dilemma arises when he decides to change hairstyles. Although forming dreadlocks is rather painless, pulling them apart may involve some discomfort.

Love, like dreadlocks, results in the bonding together of two hearts. This is pretty cool...as long as both hearts desire to stay in the relationship. Bonding two hearts into one can be rather painless, however, pulling those hearts apart can cause great pain. Any time a person decides to cut out of a relationship, at least one member of that relationship tends to be affected for quite some time. A broken heart is hard to mend. But God is able to heal the broken hearted!

The devil loves to set people up for a broken heart. He will use the world to tell you love is cheap and should be taken lightly. This lie is designed to leave you dreadlocked to pain, guilt, and regret. He wants to keep you bound to the past. But God, who is rich in mercy, will teach you that true love is valuable and should be handled with care. God is able to heal pain, remove guilt, and provide hope for tomorrow! I'm sure

21

you have had many opportunities to hear what the rest of the world has to say about love. Now you have a right to know what God says. Throughout this book, you will discover answers to the following questions:

- **What does God say about sex?**
- **What does God say about dating?**
- **What does God say about marriage?**

I pray God's truth will empower you to have an extremely AWESOME "ONE LOVE" experience!

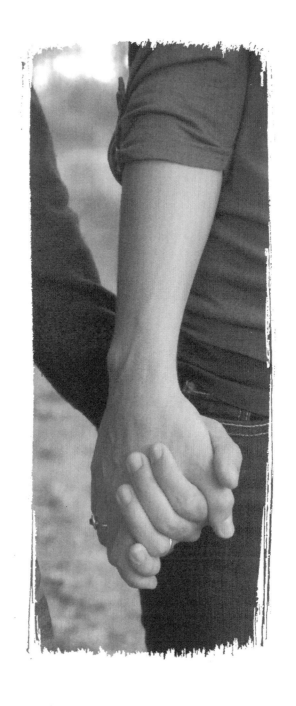

PART ONE:

WHAT DOES GOD SAY ABOUT SEX?

CHAPTER ONE

The Power of Sex!

"...but if they cannot exercise self-control, let them marry. For it is *better to marry than to burn with passion.*"
I Corinthians 7:9 NKJV

In Jamaica there is a beautiful plant called "ackee." Its bright yellow-orange color captures the attention of people who pass by its tree. The ackee plant can be prepared to eat in a variety of ways. During mission trips to Jamaica, I have eaten ackee. I remember the first experience I had with this strange food. After I stuffed my face, my Jamaican hosts decided to let me in on a little secret. They said, "If the plant is eaten at the wrong time, it is poisonous and can kill a person." WHAT?! I thought, "That would have been good to know *before* I put it into my body!" My friends assured me that the plant was ripe and I had nothing to worry about. Fortunately, I made it home alive and my ackee experience turned out well.

Sex is like the ackee plant. Experienced at the wrong time, sex has the power to consume a person's heart, mind, and body. *Brief euphoric passion is followed by the long lasting venom of guilt.* Ironically, the same venom that produces guilt also produces a destructive craving for more sex. More sex leads to more guilt and MORE poor decisions.

> EXPERIENCED AT THE WRONG TIME, SEX HAS THE POWER TO CONSUME A PERSON'S HEART, MIND, AND BODY.

EXPERIENCES SHARED AT
ONE LOVE CONFERENCES

"I became sexually active in my teens (and) pregnant at the age of 17. When my friends were headed off to college, I was preparing to become a mother. (I) found myself in a marriage that never should have happened. I ended this marriage after one year. I was 19, with a one year old child, living at home with my parents, and looking for a job without any skills. I was an adult but had to follow my mother's rules...there are prices to pay for our bad choices...I was remarried at 20. It didn't occur to me to ask God who I should marry or if I should marry at all. I was in that marriage for 27 years. I could not have more children because of an STD...the infection had scarred my fallopian tubes shut...I had four ectopic pregnancies after that...I wanted so badly to have a child that my family would welcome...I am in my third marriage..."

--Kathy

"Having been conceived by way of an adulterous affair, being bounced around as an infant, and not knowing the identity of my biological parents until much later in life, I was lacking a solid role model regarding sexual morality. I learned about 'the facts of life' on the streets of my neighborhood...I was exposed to pornography when I was in the 6th grade by a dirty old man that lived up the street from me. Another kid and I would go visit him at his junk yard business and he would share pornographic magazines with us...This led to a decade of sexual immorality beginning in high school until my late 20's, when I met my first wife...My first wife and I had sex on our first date...We lived together for 2 years and were married. The beauty that God had meant for us to save was so tarnished that we went to bed on our wedding night too exhausted to make love. By then it wasn't a big deal. This set the tone for our marriage. Later in our marriage, long after the intimacy had gone, I confessed to my first wife that I had cheated on her before we were married with a one night stand while on a business trip. I also confessed that due to the fact that we had not had a sexual experience together in nearly 2 years, that I had hired a prostitute. A year later, after 7 years of marriage, we were divorced."

--Michael

When I was a junior in high school I began to mess around with girls. In fact, just that year I had done the "True Love Waits" thing and was trying to keep to it...The problem came when the people I wanted to associate myself with in high school didn't exactly live in a way that matched up with the lifestyle I had grown accustomed to...I had begun to toy with things that weren't all the way, but were definitely pushing the limits. By the time I was a senior, I was heavy in to partying, smoking and drinking...My limits with girls, well, there weren't really any...The summer after I graduated a friend of mine and I decided to have a private party with two other girls at one of the girls' house. Her dad was out of town...We spent the entire time drinking and making out. That was until Saturday night. We all had a little too much to drink, and the one girl that I had been with all weekend said she was tired and asked if I would come lay down with her. That was the biggest mistake in my life. Instead of laying there and falling asleep we ended up having sex...I quickly got sick to my stomach... What had I been doing these last couple of years? What about that commitment from my junior year?...

continued next page

You see, the devastation to me was not that night, but 3 years down the road when I had to tell my then fiancé that she would not be my first on our wedding night. It nearly broke me in half. In fact, the feelings I had telling her that night were worse than what I had felt when I lost my virginity. This in no way plays down the seriousness of what I had done, but shows that my sin did not just affect that night, but my future as well.

--Brad

God's Word tells the true story of two lovers who were enticed by the beauty of a certain fruit. After passionately indulging in the fruit, Adam and Eve realized something was terribly wrong. What they had eaten was more poisonous than any fruit in history! This fruit was so destructive that its poison would be passed from generation to generation throughout time. Oh, how they must have longed for God to reverse time so they could make the right choice. But time stops for no man. The damage was done. Sin entered the world through one man, named Adam. It would take the perfect man named Jesus Christ to defeat sin for mankind.

Sex, at the wrong time, is similar to Adam and Eve's forbidden fruit. After passionately indulging, you will realize something is terribly wrong. You will be poisoned with guilt and lust (a destructive craving for sex).

But wait a minute! *There is good news! God does not*

intend for sex to be destructive! He is not out to steal from us. *He is the one who created this gift.* That same Ackee plant that is able to bring destruction is also able to provide nourishment. It all depends on eating the fruit at the right time. Although the power of sex can bring destruction, it all depends on the timing.

SEX AT THE RIGHT TIME, HAS THE POWER TO BOND TWO HEARTS IN AN EXTREMELY AWESOME WAY!

You see, *sex at the right time, has the power to bond two hearts in an extremely awesome way!* The important question is, "**When is the right time to experience sex?**"

CHAPTER TWO

The Time For Sex!

*"And they were both naked, the man and his wife,
and were not ashamed."*
Genesis 2:25

God desires the very best for us. He wants sex to be an extremely awesome experience. As the scripture above shows us, the man and woman were *naked* and were *not ashamed*! *God created* Adam and Eve! *GOD CREATED SEX!*

There is a book in the Bible called, *Song of Solomon*. This book describes the relationship between a man and woman in love. In chapter 8, verses 3-4, the bride says, "His left hand is under my head, and his right hand embraces me. I charge you, O daughters of Jerusalem, do not stir up nor awaken love until it pleases." Since the Bible teaches *"All Scripture is inspired by God, and is useful to teach us what is true..." II Timothy 3:16 NLT,* we can understand that *sex is not bad!* It is something that *God created* for a man and woman to enjoy when the time is right! According to the word of God, there are three requirements that must be met in order for a person to be qualified to experience sex. They are as follows:

- independence
- marriage
- oneness

INDEPENDENCE
"Therefore a man shall *leave his father and mother..."*
Genesis 2:24

God's word teaches that the first step in becoming qualified for sex is to become independent of Dad & Mom. Let's take a closer look.

> "Therefore a man shall leave his mother and be joined to his wife, and they shall become one flesh. And they were both naked, the man and his wife, and were not ashamed. "
>
> Genesis 2:24-25

Notice the last sentence of the scripture says, "And they were both naked, the man and his wife, and were not ashamed." Cool! The end result of God's plan is man and woman both get to enjoy the pleasure of sex! Now, look at the first sentence. It begins with the phrase, "...a man shall leave his father and mother..." Here, we see the first requirement in becoming qualified to experience sex.

To leave his father and mother means a man no longer needs Dad & Mom to provide for his needs. He is at a point in life where he is able and willing to work a full-time job, pay his own bills, and provide his own place to live. This is what it means to be independent.

Notice it is the man's responsibility to be the leader. God does not tell the woman to leave her parents and pursue a husband. He tells the man to take a leadership role in initiating the whole deal.

Some people think that this concept makes women appear less important than men. Nothing could be more untrue! God didn't take a bone from Adam's foot to make Eve. If he had, Adam might have thought he could walk all over her. God didn't take a bone from Adam's head to make Eve. If he had, Adam might have cowered before her. God took a bone from Adam's side so that both man and woman could stand beside each other as partners in life! Men and women are of equal value! The reality that we are different magnifies our equality. Being different causes us to be more dependent upon one another. If men and women were the same, one of us would not be necessary! **Think about it.**

Have you ever seen a living person who had a head, but not a body? Of course not! A head without a body is incomplete! Likewise, men without women are incomplete. A man is not more important than a woman. He simply has a different set of responsibilities.

God has given the man a leadership responsibility. In order for him to do the best job possible, he desperately needs the woman to partner with him. Ladies, the best way you can help a guy to be a great leader is to respect the role that God has given him. If a man does not have the woman's respect, he is incomplete.

Having a leadership role does not make man the center of the universe! In Ephesians 5, Paul explains how God expects a husband to love his wife! God uses words like, "...gave Himself up...sanctify...cherish..." to describe the way that Jesus loves His followers. Paul explains that men are supposed to love women the same way that Jesus loves His followers!

Guys, that means we need to be willing to sacrifice our own selfish desires in order to serve her needs, rather than expecting her to be a slave to our every desire. That means we need to honor her by helping her keep herself pure for marriage, not pushing her to do things that are wrong. That means we need to treat her respectfully by cherishing her life, not talking abusively to her. God desires men to assume the responsibility of lead partner while He desires women to assume the role of supportive partner. Until a young man is at a point in life when he is prepared to be the lead partner, he is not prepared to experience sex!

Until a woman is at a point in life when she is prepared to be the supportive partner, she is not prepared to experience sex. But remember, there are two more qualifications in addition to independence. *All three qualifications must be met before sex can be experienced in an extremely awesome way!*

MARRIAGE
"...(a man) shall be *joined* to his wife..."
Genesis 2:24

The second step in becoming qualified for sex is marriage. When a man and woman publicly pledge to commit to one another spiritually, emotionally, and physically, they become married. The Bible says in Matthew 19:6, "...*what God has joined together, let not man separate.*" This means that God's plan is for a husband and wife to be joined together until death separates them. No one should ever enter into marriage thinking, "If I am not happy, I'll just get a divorce." According to the Bible, marriage is not just a legal agreement, but a *holy joining* together of two people in the eyes of God.

So, a marriage ceremony is all it takes for a man and woman to become qualified to experience sex, right? WRONG! Many people, who have no desire to honor

God, get married. In fact, people who don't even *know* each other have wedding ceremonies that cheapen the beauty of marriage.

You have probably seen videos of people dressed in crazy costumes, participating in a wedding led by an Elvis impersonator. There are still others who do not have Jesus at the center of their relationship. They are certainly not serving Him through a local church, yet they want to have a "church" wedding. They may even expect the pastor to pronounce God's blessing upon their masquerade. All too often, I fear that God and His church are being used as good luck charms or cheap substitutes for God's plan!

> TRUTH, CHRISTIANS ARE ABLE TO EXPERIENCE SEX TO THE FULL POTENTIAL OF GOD'S DESIGN!

Marriage is designed to honor God. When a man and woman are truly joined together in the eyes of God, they become eligible to experience sex in the most extremely awesome way! The world seems to believe that Christians are *not* allowed to enjoy sex! In truth, Christians are able to experience sex to the full potential of God's design! But wait a minute! Simply going through the motions of a wedding ceremony does not qualify you to experience sex in the most incredible way. There is still one final step in experiencing sex without shame. This final step is called, "oneness."

ONENESS

"...(man and wife) shall become *one* flesh."
Genesis 2:24

The third step in becoming qualified for guilt-free sex is called oneness. To become "one flesh" is to share life together.

There *are* people who have met the first two qualifications, but have never experienced oneness! These people are able to provide for their own needs independently. They have been married (joined). However, they have never truly given themselves to their husband or wife. There *are* people who have open marriage agreements. That means they are legally married, but have agreed to have sexual relations with other people.

Some people get married as a financial partnership. Two politicians may get married in order to help one another's career without truly loving one another. There are even people who get married, gain access to one another's bank accounts, cars, and property, but never move into the same house.

According to God's word *none of the above people* are qualified to experience sex in the purest way. The marriage union includes every area of life. A husband and wife who are "one flesh" share money, possessions, struggles, dreams, children, conversation...*EVERYTHING!*

ALL THREE
QUALIFICATIONS
MUST BE MET
BEFORE SEX CAN
BE EXPERIENCED
IN AN EXTREMELY
AWESOME WAY!

- INDEPENDENCE
- MARRIAGE
- ONENESS

We will talk more about this in the next section called *"What will I do about dating?"* Meanwhile, remember God's plan. The right time for sex is when a man and woman have met *all three* requirements: *independence, marriage, and oneness.*

CHAPTER THREE

The Combination For Sex!

"Therefore a *man* shall...be joined to his *wife*..."
Genesis 2:24

In Genesis 2:24-25, God clearly states that He intends for marriage to include "a" man and "a" woman. The word "man" means MALE! The word "woman" means FEMALE! So...we can clearly see that biblical marriage is between one MAN and one WOMAN. You may be wondering, *"Is it a sin to be gay?"*

First of all, let it be understood that God loves people, regardless of the lifestyle they live. The Bible teaches, *"God so loved the world that He gave His one and only*

Son, that whoever believes in him shall not perish but have eternal life" (John 3:16 NIV). God hates sin, but He loves sinners. His word says, *"whoever will call on the name of the Lord will be saved"* (Romans 10:13 NASB). When a person trusts in Jesus Christ as Savior and Lord, there is absolutely *no sin* that God is not able to forgive in that person's life.

The Bible does make it clear that homosexuality is contrary to God's will. Scripture tells of people

> "...who exchanged the truth of God for a lie...For this reason God gave them up to vile passions. For even their women exchanged the natural use for what is against nature. Likewise also, the men, leaving the natural use of the woman, burned in their lust for one another, men with men committing what is shameful, and receiving in themselves the penalty of their error which was due."
>
> Romans 1:24-27

So, what about people who are born homosexual? Why would God create someone with a tendency to do something that He has already determined is sinful?

These are good questions that do have clear answers. The key word is "tendency." All people are born with tendencies. God created Adam and Eve with the tendency to live according to His will. When they chose to disobey God, sin entered into the world. In that moment, mankind's tendency changed. As a result, people are now born with a tendency toward sin. Specific people tend to be tempted more strongly in specific areas. One person may have a tendency toward drug addiction. Another may have a tendency toward violence. Still another might tend toward self-pity.

When a person accepts Jesus Christ as Savior and Lord, God gives him/her new tendencies. This is called the "new nature." The new nature tends to do what is right, giving us victory over our old nature to sin. Jesus died and resurrected that people might have victory over sin. God does not condemn *anyone* who will confess their sin and invite Him to change his/her tendencies.

CHAPTER FOUR

The Process of Sex!

"...when desire has conceived, it gives birth to sin;
and sin, when it is full-grown, brings forth death."
James 1:15

Sex is like bowling! Bowling is a process. It begins with the eyes as the bowler studies the pins and plans his approach. It progresses as he physically moves forward. It rapidly picks up speed as he releases the ball down the lane. Once the ball is rolling, it is *extremely* hard to stop the process. Imagine some lunatic slipping and sliding down the lane as he tries to catch the ball. Can you say, "LOSER?" It would be better not to bowl than to try and stop a rolling ball.

Sex is progressive. It begins with the eyes as one person studies another. In Matthew 5:28, God's word says, "...whoever looks at a woman to lust for her has already committed adultery with her in his heart." Proverbs 6:25 says, "Do not lust after (an evil woman's) beauty in your heart, nor let her allure you with her eyelids." Sex progresses as one person plans his approach.

The whole process picks up speed with physical activity. Once physical activity begins, it is *extremely* hard to stop the process. It would be better to stop before physical activity begins. Some of the most miserable people in the world are those who have decided not to have sex right now but don't understand *"the process!"* They continually start the process, get in the middle of it, then try to stop a rolling ball. Man, that has to be miserable because **the process is designed to be completed!**

Remember, God created sex. He has never done anything halfway. Sex is powerful because God intends it to be an extremely awesome experience that is extremely hard to forget. When two people engage in sex, their hearts and emotions are also engaged. **The sexual experience is designed to be remembered!**

So...whatever emotions are involved will be very hard to forget! Whatever images are viewed will be very hard to delete! God gave sex to husbands and wives to be an unforgettable expression of their love for one another. God wants husbands and wives to experience the full pleasure of sex, so He created a *process* that would lead to fulfillment. That's right! Sex is not just one act. It is an entire process which leads to completion. If you are committed to saving sex for marriage, *you need to be committed to abstaining from the entire process!*

> IF YOU ARE COMMITTED TO SAVING SEX FOR MARRIAGE, YOU NEED TO BE COMMITTED TO ABSTAINING FROM THE ENTIRE PROCESS!

A lot of people seem to think that sex is on the edge of an imaginary line. They like to see how close they can get to the edge without going over. That approach leaves them frustrated and anxious. *Since sex is a process*, their strength eventually breaks down and they end up falling over the line *they vowed they would never cross!* This is the wrong approach. Instead of testing the limits and getting as close to the line as possible, a follower of Jesus Christ should see how *far away from the edge* he/she can stay. In other words, don't see how much you can "do" and not go "all the way!" See how much of the process you can save for marriage!

Don't expect to repeatedly start the process and then be able to stop it suddenly! *Be prepared!* Set up some safety boundaries for yourself. Set high expectations and associate yourself with people who share those expectations. Remember, you can take a pill to protect yourself from pregnancy. You can use a

49

condom to protect yourself from disease. But what will protect you from the heartbreak of sexual sin? Why not protect your heart by honoring God's principles? **Save the entire process for marriage!**

CHAPTER FIVE

The Gift of Forgiveness!

"Therefore, if anyone is in Christ, he is a new creation;
old things have passed away;
behold, all things have become new."
II Corinthians 5:17

At this point you could be thinking, "Oh man. I wish someone had told me this *before* I got so involved. What can I do now? I've already messed up. If I could only turn back time." You cannot turn back time. However, you *can* turn your past over to God! You can turn away from sin. You *can* turn *to* a new style of love. And best of all...*you can experience forgiveness.*

FORGIVENESS:
AN EXTREME GIFT

"I grew up surrounded by the love of a Christian family. I accepted Christ as my Savior when I was a young girl. My world was flipped upside down in high school when my family was faced with a series of shattering events. As a result I became filled with anger, pain and confusion. Rather than turning to the Lord, I relied on other people and things as an escape. I ended up on a painful path as a teenage pregnancy, which later followed with severe depression, drinking and rape. I never intended to be the person and parent I had become. I couldn't find the strength to forgive myself, or dare to ask for forgiveness from the Savior I knew as a child. Later, in my mid-twenties, severe depression left me too weak to care for my daughter and myself. Weary and broken, I cried out to the Lord to forgive and heal me. If He would just forgive me I was willing to trust Him to provide the love I longed for...

continued on the next page

The Lord worked in me changing my brokenness to beauty. He mended a failed relationship with my daughter's father and restored our family when he accepted Christ as his Savior. Through all of life's challenges, Jesus is the one who never changes. Because of Christ's love, I am forgiven. Because of His forgiveness, we are living an amazing adventure with more to come."

--Brooke

At the beginning I told you about my life and...how these facts related to abstinence. I wanted to have a large family. I have one child...I could not have more children because of a STD. When I should have been attending college, I was raising a child. Here's the good news...When you know you are a child of God,....you won't need another person to make you feel loved...you won't make decisions in your life so you'll feel loved. Always remember that God loves you unfailingly and unconditionally...You are so fortunate to know this now, in this time of your life...He has great plans for you. Just ask Him, He'll let you know what road to take. Human wisdom and human desire can achieve human results. But praying to God produces divine results.

--Kathy

During the pain of a failed marriage, God brought a man into my life that challenged me and led me to commit to living the Christian life. After nearly three years of abstinence, God brought into my life a companion. She had also gone through a failed marriage. We agreed at the beginning of our relationship to try it God's way. We had a courtship of 18 months and saved our intimacy for our wedding night. We will soon be celebrating our 10th wedding anniversary. Our intimacy has only deepened over the years...God's way is the best option. He knows because He made us."

--Michael

"...God forgave me, and my fiancé did as well. We are married now...that Saturday night still haunts me, but to this day I know that it is past."

--Brad

The entire reason Jesus came died and rose again was to pay for the sins of the world. That means *every* sin. Whatever you have done, Jesus has already taken the punishment for it in advance. All you must do to experience forgiveness is to admit that what you have been doing has been displeasing to God.

If you have already invited Jesus Christ to forgive your sinful tendencies and become Lord of your life, your salvation is secure. You just need to ask your Lord to forgive you and turn away from your previous actions. You may need to talk to your parents, pastor, or youth minister for guidance in breaking some of the habits you have been involved with. But you need to remember that Jesus has come off the cross. He finished paying for your sins. To hold on to them is to question Jesus' ability to pay your debt. Let go today and return to a right relationship with Jesus.

If you have never invited Jesus Christ to forgive your sins and become Lord of your life, you need to know what in the world it means for Him to be Lord. If you would like to know RIGHT NOW how to be forgiven of sin and have Him in your life, I invite you to skip to page 95. Once you have read the section entitled "RAP UP", you will want to come back and finish the book. In fact, I am sure the rest of the book will become even more interesting to you once you have read the end! So what are you waiting for? Read page 95!

PART TWO:

- - - - - - - -

WHAT DOES GOD SAY ABOUT DATING?

CHAPTER SIX

House Cat Gone Wild!

A house cat sits and looks through the sliding glass door. He curiously, observes tantalizing insects wiggling across the patio. He licks his chops as birds land a few feet away from him. For a moment, he forgets he is detained and bangs his head on the glass door as he lunges toward a bird. Shaking his head, he suddenly notices something that causes his eyes to expand into little saucers. It's...a female cat...a girl!

Never has he seen any creature so fascinating! So begins the quest. Week after week, Mr. House Cat watches the girl next door. Day after day he wonders what it would be like to get out and play with the neighbor's cat. Then one day it happens! The sliding door opens. The house cat hears a voice say, "Go!" Slowly he ventures through the front yard, across the street and into the neighbor's yard. The two cats shyly approach one another, ready to flinch spastically and scurry away in several directions if anything freaky happens.

Eventually, they become familiar and develop a wonderful relationship. At the end of each day, the house cat hears his master call him home. The owner typically dangles an enticing piece of string and says, "Here kitty, kitty." Since a cat's fascination with inanimate objects seems to be much larger that its attention span, he is immediately captivated and slinks toward the house as if to stalk and conquer the deadly piece of string. Eventually, he strolls into the house and settles in for a lazy evening.

Each morning, the cat is poised and ready for the magical sliding glass door to open. His main objective, the female cat across the street! Over time, he becomes less cautious.

One dreadful day, the glass opens. He darts across the yard, eyes passionately fixed on the female cat. Though he runs swiftly, time seems to move in slow motion. His hair gently sways in the breeze...her eyes slowly flutter...As his paws softly land upon the pavement, BAM! A car blind-sides him. The next day, he lays in the basement, barely able to move. As he licks his wounds he wonders, *"How could something so good turn out so bad?"*

This is how dating can feel! You spend your life in your parent's house. As you get older you begin to notice the opposite sex in a different way. You begin to wonder what it would be like to spend more time with her/him. Finally, Mom and Dad set you free. You venture out into the world of dating. Next thing you know, you are all caught up in it. What a great freedom...to be a teenager in love! Then, all of the sudden you get blind-sided! She dumps you...you see him with another girl...you break up. You lay in bed that night wondering, *"How can something so good turn out so bad?"*

If you have ever experienced the pain of a break up, you may have taken steps to guard yourself against future hurt. Some people guard their hearts by avoiding commitments. Others guard their hearts by beating others to the punch. They will use a relationship for selfish benefits and break up the relationship suddenly.

Perhaps you are wondering how to avoid the risk of pain in dating. GOOD NEWS: There is a plan that will reduce your risk and keep you from hurting others as well. There are two main journeys you can take in regard to romance. The journey people typically choose is commonly known as *dating*. The other option is an extreme experience called *courtship*.

I believe that courtship is the best and most biblical choice. I understand that the term may sound old school. I also recognize that some readers are not ready to take this extreme journey, even though they are ready to raise their standards. Therefore, it is my desire to show how the principles of courtship can be infused into the existing world of dating. Hopefully, this will encourage every reader to move steadily toward a more pure love life while challenging the more radical reader to plunge into the river of freedom that flows within the banks of courtship.

THE MOST IMPORTANT ISSUE IS NOT WHAT YOU CALL THESE PRINCIPLES, BUT THAT YOU LIVE THEM OUT IN A WAY THAT HONORS GOD.

I will spend the rest of this chapter introducing God's principles for dating, romance, courtship, or whatever you choose to call it. *The most important issue is not what you call these principles, but that you live them out in a way that honors God.* If you really want your love life to reach its extreme potential, you will need to honor the following principles:

- The Father's Presence
- The Father's Prescription
- The Father's Plan

CHAPTER SEVEN

Honor the Father's Presence!

"Children, obey your parents in the Lord... that it may be well with you...And you, *fathers*, do not provoke your children..."
Ephesians 6:1-4

Sons and daughters need the presence of a wise and loving father in order to help them make healthy decisions about dating. A strong father figure equips a boy with a proper understanding of how to love a woman. Such a father also equips his daughter with a proper understanding of how she should be treated by a man who says he loves her. In a healthy father-daughter relationship, Dad will also offer security for his daughter by establishing clear expectations with any boy who wants to date his daughter.

A friend of mine, who has married off two daughters, provides an incredible example of "daughter security." A few years ago, a boy wanted to take his oldest daughter to a school dance. This father had worked throughout his daughter's childhood to establish a strong and loving presence in her life. He had conversations with her about the day when some boy would want to take her out on a date. It was understood that the boy would be expected to ask the father's permission for a date with his daughter. It was also understood that Dad would talk privately with him before entrusting his most prized possession into the care of another man.

It was no surprise when my friend requested a meeting with the boy. During that meeting, the father communicated that he did not like the term, "dating." He told the boy that he did not want to call the situation a date, but he would agree to let him *chaperone* his daughter. He explained, "As a chaperone, I will be entrusting you to stand in my place and protect my daughter as if you were *me*. Do you understand this?" The eager boy affirmed his willingness to do this.

What followed was an act of genius and a demonstration of true love. The father further explained, "Let me make sure you understand. If my daughter was with me, I would make sure nobody hurt her. I would die defending her. If anyone tried to give her drugs, I would stop them. And if anyone should try to steal my daughter's purity, I would die to keep it from happening. You son, will be acting in *my* place. Are you willing to defend her honor the same way *I* would defend her honor?" After a long pause, the young man humbly replied, "Yes sir. I understand. I will protect your daughter's honor."

This approach helped both the daughter and the boy become aware of the most important key to a healthy dating situation. That key is *the father's presence!* My friend wanted his presence to be felt during his daughter's date. But there is an even deeper...more powerful principle that he was really trying to establish.

In the life of a Christian, there is always a Father present. Even if a girl does not have a good Dad, God wants her and the guy she is with to remember that *He* is in the car. *He* is at the party. *He is everywhere*, sees everything, and desires the very best. He has already given His life for His child through the crucifixion of Jesus Christ. He expects His child to be loved and respected with the same love that Christ demonstrated on the cross.

> IN THE LIFE OF A CHRISTIAN, THERE IS ALWAYS A FATHER PRESENT.

Dads are protectors entrusted by *God!* Yes, a guy should ask permission from a girl's father before dating her. Parents are the #1 people that God has made responsible to protect their sons and daughters. Fathers have been entrusted by God to lead, serve and protect the whole family. Ephesians 6:4 says, *"...fathers, do not provoke your children to wrath, but bring them up in the training and admonition of the Lord."* This verse communicates the power that a father has to bless or curse his children. One of the father's responsibilities is to ensure that his family is trained in God's ways.

Girls should honor the father's position. Hopeful boyfriends should also honor the father's position. Even if the father is a "bad Dad," the dating couple can challenge him to be a better father just by honoring his role in his daughter's life. Remember, until the boy becomes a man, gets a full-time job, marries the girl and the two become one flesh, God wants her *dad to be the main man in her life!*

But what if you don't have a strong Christian father in your life? God wants you to know that He has not forgotten you. Through Jesus Christ, you can learn to know the presence of Father God in your life. Your earthly Dad is really the one missing out on an opportunity to demonstrate God's love and protection for you. That truly is unfortunate.

But that doesn't mean you have to miss out. As you read your Bible and pray, ask God to put healthy father figures in your life. A grandfather, uncle, big brother, etc. it is not the person's biological relationship to you that matters most. It is his ability to represent God's love in your life.

You may be thinking, "Hey! What about us guys?" The Father factor is just as important for you. You need to recognize God as your ultimate Father because you need someone to teach you how to treat a woman. You too, need to be reading your Bible and praying for God to put strong Christian men in your life who can teach you how to provide, love, and care for a woman of God. He can make this happen, but you need to talk to Him about it.

Ultimately, guys and girls alike must learn to lean on God as Father. There will likely come a day when even the greatest Dad will not be available. No man can be everywhere...all the time...for us. *But God can.* He is not pretend like Santa Claus. He is not somewhere out there keeping His distance. *He is very real and wants to be up close in your life as Father.*

Why not ask Him, right now, to help you learn His presence?

CHAPTER EIGHT

Honor the Father's Prescription!

"Therefore a man shall leave his father and mother and be joined to his wife, and they shall become one flesh."
Genesis 2:24-25

Imagine you are the leader of an incredible band. For the past two years you have poured yourself into music. You have spent endless hours rehearsing your band and developing your skills as a musician. There was a time when you wondered if you would ever get a real gig. Friends used to joke that you would never make it past your mom's garage. Finally you are beginning to get a lot of opportunities to play. A major record company has listened to your demo and wants to talk about a contract. But just when it seems like your ship has come in your lead guitarist informs you that he must quit the band. After the shock wears off, you decide to interview some people to play in your band. As the entire band gathers for the first interview, in walks "Johnny Metal." He looks like the ultimate rocker. He has the right hair and the right clothes. He carries the coolest, most expensive guitar you have ever seen. There is no doubt this guy has the look of a band member. The question is, "Can he play?" After all, looks can be deceiving. Before you take a risk on this guy, he needs to demonstrate his talent.

Great bands don't hire members just because they look good. Band members need to meet certain standards. They must demonstrate stellar skills on their instrument. They must meet the expectations of creativity and compatibility with the rest of the band. They also have to demonstrate a level of commitment that will serve to make the entire band successful. He must show that he has earned the right to be in the band. A great band will not waste precious time working with a pretender.

ONCE WE ARE AWARE OF HIS PRESCRIPTION, WE ARE ABLE TO AUDITION THOSE WHO ARE INTERESTED IN OUR HEARTS.

Someone who is looking for true love should not waste precious time in an immature relationship. Fortunately, God has provided a very clear prescription for choosing somebody to love. *Once we are aware of His prescription, we are able to audition those who are interested in our hearts.* The following three principles, found in Genesis 2:24-25, are part of God's prescription:

1. **Choose someone who is responsible!**
2. **Choose someone who is committed!**
3. **Choose someone who is unselfish!**

CHOOSE SOMEONE WHO IS RESPONSIBLE!

"A *man* shall leave his father and mother..."
Genesis 2:24

In this verse, to "leave father and mother" means to become responsible. God clearly expects the man to take a leadership role in being a responsible provider. This means he no longer depends on his parents to pay for his groceries, car payment, insurance, or other basic expenses. He has left the mother bird's nest and is capable of living on his own.

This principle alone eliminates most teenagers in the U.S.A from even considering the possibility of participating in sex. Remember, God does not just make up rules to keep us from having fun. There are practical reasons for the expectations He gives.

Why do you think it is important to God that a man and woman be financially responsible before considering sex? **Think about it.**

Typically sex is accompanied by the possibility of a baby! If two people are going to explore sexual activity, they need to remember that sex leads to babies. Many couples who are committed to "safe sex" have ended up with unexpected pregnancies.

Since pregnancy is not the baby's fault and God desires for babies to live, it is important that the couple who produces the baby is able to provide and tend to the child's needs. *How many teenage boys, who are experiencing sex, have demonstrated this level of responsibility? How many teen girls, who are sexually active, are truly ready to be a mother?*

These questions are a good "throw back" to our previous chapter, *"What does God say about sex?"*

But this chapter is not primarily about sex. It is about choosing someone who knows how to take good care of your *heart* and honor you as a child of God. Even if a dating couple is committed to saving sex for marriage, the principle of choosing someone who is responsible is extremely important.

For instance, any guy who wants to take one of God's daughters out on a date needs to be responsible enough to provide transportation and pay her way. He also needs to be responsible enough to put himself in harm's way if necessary to protect her. This does not mean that the girl cannot drive or pay for the date occasionally. However, this is primarily the guy's responsibility. He should be prepared and expecting to act accordingly. If your date is too young to hold down a full-time job, he at least needs to show that he is working to *become* the kind of man who will be a responsible provider.

For teenage girls, a good way to decide if a boy meets this standard is to consider how he treats the responsibilities that he does have. If he is a student, does he treat his schoolwork with the same level of responsibility you would want him to treat your relationship? If he has a part-time job, does his boss respect him as an employee? Does he have chores at home that his parents expect him to do? If he is not responsible toward his parents, he will not continue to be responsible in your relationship. Count on it.

These principles apply to girls as well. Guys, if you are set on becoming a man of God, you should look for a young lady who demonstrates responsibility in her life. If she is overly demanding of her parents' attention, she might just be overly demanding of your attention. If she is not responsible with her schoolwork, chores, etc...she will probably be irresponsible in your relationship.

You may be wondering, *"What if the guy is able to provide? What if the guy and girl are both responsible, mature, hard-working people? Does this mean they are ready for a relationship?"* Not necessarily! Remember, there are two more character traits included in God's prescription. All three are vital in finding somebody to love.

CHOOSE SOMEONE WHO IS COMMITTED!

"..and be joined to his wife..."
(Genesis 2:24)

To be "joined" means to cling to one another like skin clings to bone. This implies the deepest level of commitment to one another. Bones depend on skin to protect them. Skin depends on bone to give it support. One without the other becomes weak and vulnerable. In finding somebody to love, you need someone who will be committed to protecting and supporting you. You do not need someone who will tear away from you and leave you feeling week and vulnerable.

If someone is interested in having your heart, make them audition in the area of commitment. If he is on a sports team, does he show up for practice on time? Does he practice all year and then quit just when the team is depending on him for a big game? If she has a job, does she strive to be a dependable employee or does she call in sick just so she can hang out with friends? If someone treats such important commitments this way, they will most likely treat their commitment to you the same way.

The ultimate promise of commitment is a wedding ceremony. This is the day that witnesses gather to listen to a man and woman promise themselves exclusively to one another. The promise is to forsake all other romantic relationships until death.

A lot of people these days want the benefits of love without the commitment. People don't mind living together and enjoying one another's company, but find it inconvenient to make a life-long promise. Such a relationship is not a "joined" relationship where two people are clinging to one another like skin to bones. It is more like a hat that you can take off and cast aside when it gets old and boring.

A real man of God will commit to his bride above everyone and everything else. He will cling to her like skin to bones, protecting her at all costs. He will not indulge in the benefits of a marriage relationship without making a real marriage commitment. A real woman of God will take commitment very seriously so that the man she marries can trust that she will support him like bone supports skin. If you choose to date, don't just date anyone. Reserve yourself for a person who is demonstrating strong commitment in their responsibilities.

CHOOSE SOMEONE WHO IS UNSELFISH!
"...they shall become *one flesh*..."
Genesis 2:24

In order to become one flesh, a man and woman must share everything they have with one another. That's why wedding vows include the statement, "I promise all of my worldly goods..." A real man of God is willing to share everything he has with his lady. A real woman of God is willing to share all that she has with her man.

Each one's mindset will change from "my" car to "our" car...from "my" house to "our" house...from "my" money to our money. True love is willing to turn large amounts of "my" time into more of "our" time together. An unselfish man is willing to share his heart with the woman he loves. If he is upset about something, he will be willing to *talk* to her about it rather than hide his feelings from her for long periods of time. An unselfish woman will look for ways to communicate effectively with the man she loves.

A couple who has become "one flesh" places one another's needs above everyone and everything else including sports, friends, and video games. The only relationship that should *ever* come between a husband and wife is his/her relationship with God.

You might wonder, "But if I am really in love with someone, is it right to put God before them?" Yes, because a right relationship with God actually enables you to love others *more* than you could without God in your life. God *is* love. The closer you get to Him, the more love you have to give.

There will be times when you need time alone with God. But once that time has been spent, the best way to honor God is by honoring the marriage commitment. Even if you are not yet married, you can begin honoring your future marriage through the way you approach dating.

You should never marry someone who has not demonstrated that he/she is:

1. **Responsible**
2. **Committed**
3. **Unselfish**

In practicing for marriage, you should not date someone who is lacking these qualities.

Ladies, make those guys *audition* for a position in your life. If you have not had time to observe the way he handles responsibilities, commitments, and relationships, do not waste time finding out the hard way!

Guys, if you want to have a real woman, then you must earn that right by becoming a real man. This mainly comes through your personal relationship with Jesus Christ.

As you grow in your relationship with Christ through prayer and Bible reading, He will make you into the real deal. By spending more time with God and less time playing the dating game, you will

> THE BEST ACTIONS TO TAKE IN FINDING TRUE LOVE ARE TO PRACTICE BEING RESPONSIBLE, COMMITTED, AND UNSELFISH.

actually be ready for romance sooner. It you rush love,

you will find yourself frustrated, confused, and hurt (like the house cat gone wild). In the end, you will be heart-broken, lonely and incomplete.

The best actions to take in finding true love are to practice being responsible, committed, and unselfish. If you have chores, ask God to help you do them promptly and with excellence. If you are part of a team, be the most committed one on the team. If you are blessed with cool stuff, practice sharing it with someone whose family does not have much stuff.

Most importantly, open up your Bible and practice spending time with God. At the end of this road, you are most likely to find true and lasting love.

CHAPTER NINE

The Father's Plan!

"Do not be unequally yoked together with unbelievers.
For what fellowship has righteousness with lawlessness?
And what communion has light with darkness? And
what accord has Christ with Belial (Satan?) Or what
part has a believer with an unbeliever? And what
agreement has the temple of God with idols?
For you are the temple of the living God..."
II Corinthians 6:14 NKJV

A soft drink quickly becomes flat as ice melts into it. This
is because the ice is made from water while the soft
drink has other ingredients that dominate its taste.
Have you ever noticed that water does not go flat?

Melting ice does not steal the enjoyment of a cold glass of H2O. In fact, water actually seems to taste *better* as ice melts into it.

A born-again child of God who gives his heart to someone that is not "born again," is like ice melting into a soft drink. At first the relationship seems great. It is full of *fizz* and exciting like a soft drink. But as the Christian grows closer to God, she begins to make changes in her life. Sinful behaviors of the past will become unattractive and the desire to be involved in more God-honoring activities increases.

The second person in the relationship usually becomes uncomfortable with these changes. He longs for the former lover to return and often asks her to compromise her character in order to satisfy the emptiness he feels inside. But only Jesus Christ can fill an empty soul.

Ultimately the new spirit within the Christian just does not mix with the spirit of the unbeliever. Even though a Christian might *feel* madly in love with someone who is not a Christian, his spirit is different and the two will eventually grow apart instead of closer together.

Two Christians, who are growing in their individual relationships with God, are more like a glass of ice water. Both have the Holy Spirit of God infused into their being. Since the Holy Spirit is changing both individuals, the relationship grows stronger with time. Melting ice actually *improves a glass of water!* Two believers may not always *feel* madly in love, but the

Spirit of God is able to blend their hearts together and make them pleasing in the eyes of God.

THERE IS
ONE BODY
AND ONE SPIRIT,
JUST AS YOU
WERE CALLED IN
ONE HOPE
OF YOUR CALLING;
ONE LORD,
ONE FAITH,
ONE BAPTISM;
ONE GOD
AND FATHER OF ALL,
WHO IS ABOVE ALL,
AND THROUGH ALL,
AND IN YOU ALL.

EPHESIANS 4:4-6
NKJV

PART THREE:

WHAT DOES GOD SAY ABOUT MARRIAGE?

The "Pride County" high school basketball team takes the floor. Their seven-foot center wins the opening tip and it's "GAME ON!"

Suddenly things go wrong! Two players run to the wrong end of the court. The forward runs over to the concession stand and orders a large drink. The point guard walks over and sits on the visiting team's bench and the center throws the ball to the referee! The basketball team looks foolish and the fans of Pride County begin to throw objects at their coach. Pride County is dishonored because the team has not represented them well.

There are usually two names on a basketball player's jersey, the team name and his family name. When a basketball player puts on the team jersey, everything he does represents his team. Everything he does represents the fans. Everything he does represents his family.

CHAPTER TEN

The Marriage Jersey

"...Come, I will show you the bride, the Lamb's wife..."
Revelation 21:9

The love of a husband and wife symbolize the love that Jesus has for His followers. In fact, Jesus refers to those who trust in Him as His "bride" in Revelation 21:9. When you "put on the marriage jersey," everything you do within that marriage represents Jesus Christ.

"Okay, okay" you might say. "What does marriage have to do with me? I'm just interested in dating. Can you tell me what the Bible says about dating?" Well, as far as I know, *dating is not discussed in the Bible.*

Engagement and marriage are! Dating, at its very best, is practicing how to treat the person you will one day marry.

People who are dating should be helping one another to save themselves sexually and emotionally for marriage. In this case, dating might be a healthy endeavor. On the other hand, dating that does not help two individuals save their purity for marriage is an unhealthy distraction. *When God's principles are not honored, dating becomes practice for divorce.*

Think about the way most people approach dating. Two people declare that they "belong" to one another. They symbolize this by exchanging tokens such as class rings, clothing, etc. They call themselves a "couple." They treat the relationship as if it was a marriage. But there is typically an understanding that this commitment will only last as long as "I am satisfied" or "until someone more attractive catches my attention." Then the relationship is cast aside and it is on to the next person.

INVESTMENT IN A STRONG MARRIAGE "TOMORROW" INCLUDES MAKING WISE DECISIONS ABOUT SEX, DATING, AND LOVE "TODAY."

If dating is practice for marriage, it is no wonder that so many people take their wedding vows so lightly. This approach to dating can have a strong influence on a person's future marriage commitment. The "you *belong to me until I don't feel the love any more"* model has produced a devastating divorce rate in many cultures today. An unhealthy life-style of dating has influenced thousands of people to promise in front of God and witnesses, "I will love you for better or worse, richer or poorer, in sickness and in health, as long as we both shall live" while thinking to themselves, "If my feelings change at any point, I can always get a divorce."

Since marriage represents Jesus Christ, a wise person will begin to invest in his/her future marriage in advance. *Investment in a strong marriage "tomorrow" includes making wise decisions about sex, dating, and love "today."* For some people, this could require the break up of an unhealthy dating relationship. In this situation, it may be a good idea to take a break from dating and spend a few months getting closer to Jesus. This can be very hard. The more of your heart, mind, and body you have given away, the harder it will be.

But guess what? There is no law that says, "You must have a boyfriend or girlfriend." This is something that our culture has invented. Peers, media, and well meaning adults have pressured young people into relationships that become consuming and regretful.

If you are in a consuming relationship, why not set yourself free and enjoy being young without the drama? You might just find time to hang out with friends and enjoy life in a more simple way again. Remember, dating is not marriage. Do not let someone who is not ready to fulfill the responsibilities of marriage treat you like you belong to them.

For others, investing in your future marriage may simply require a few adjustments in the dating relationship. Agreeing to give one other more space, setting boundaries and limitations on alone time, focusing more on the friendship and less on the romance are all good actions to take.

No matter what you choose to do, just remember the goal is to represent Jesus Christ more accurately both today and in your future marriage.

"RAP UP"

All of your relationships with the opposite sex involve emotional bonds. When these relationships break up, they leave emotional *and* spiritual scars. Scars are carried with you from one relationship to the next and ultimately into your future marriage.

Remember, marriage represents Jesus Christ! All of your romantic relationships ultimately represent *Jesus Christ* to this lost world. So the success of your love life boils down to this most important question:

WHAT WILL YOU DO ABOUT JESUS CHRIST?

If He is already your Lord, it is vital that you stay in tune with His voice. You need to continue to study the Bible consistently. You need to continue to talk with and listen to Him throughout each day. You need to pay attention to the biblical truths contained in this book. Most importantly, you need to remember *who you are*. You are a child of God! You are a member of the *body* of Christ! Make sure that your love life is representing Him well because the world is counting on your example to understand the love of God!

But what if you are not sure about your standing with

Jesus Christ? What if you have never made Him Lord? What if you don't even understand what that means? GREAT QUESTION! Allow me explain to you the meaning of knowing Jesus Christ as your Lord.

The Bible teaches that we are born searching for something. Isaiah 55:2 says, *"Why do you spend your wages for what does not satisfy?"*

All of your life you have been spending your "wages" (time, money, desires) in search of something that will satisfy the empty spot deep within your soul. But no matter how much "stuff" you acquire...no matter how much popularity you experience...no matter how much physical pleasure you experience...something still seems to be missing.

In Romans 3:23, the Bible says *"...for all have sinned and fall short of the glory of God..."*

God is the creator of the universe! Men and women are created in His image *Genesis 1:26-27.* That means we were created to represent and know God personally! Adam and Eve were created without sin, but they had a choice to obey or disobey God. When they chose to disobey, they lost their innocence. They immediately acquired a tendency to disobey and misrepresent God. This tendency is called sin. As descendants of Adam and Eve, we are born with that same tendency. No matter how hard we try, we just keep thinking, saying, and doing things that misrepresent God. As a result, we do not *know* God.

Later, in the book of Romans 6:23, the Bible says, *"For the wages of sin is death, but the gift of God is eternal life in Christ Jesus our Lord."*

This means that *God takes our sin very seriously.* He requires a payment to cover our sin problem. That payment is "eternal death." Without some kind of intervention from God, we are destined to live our entire lives with something missing. We are destined to miss out on true joy and fulfillment. Worst of all, we are destined to spend eternity separated from Him. The Bible even speaks of a place called Hell, which is the only option we have when we die without God in our lives. That is *bad news!* But hold on! THERE IS GOOD NEWS!!!

Romans 5:8 says, *"But God demonstrates His own love toward us, in that while we were still sinners, Christ died for us."* God has demonstrated His desire for us to know Him personally by sending His own Son, Jesus Christ, to pay for our sins.

> *"For God so loved the world that He gave His only begotten Son, that whoever believes in Him should not perish but have everlasting life. For God did not send His Son into the world to condemn the world, but that the world through Him might be saved."*
>
> John 3:16-17

The Bible reveals Jesus Christ as the Son of God, Who came to earth as the only virgin born baby in history.

This baby grew to be a child...then a teenager...then a man. Jesus experienced the temptation to sin as no other man has or ever will. Yet, He never gave in. Eventually He allowed Himself to be arrested and put to death for crimes that He never committed. Three days later, He rose from the grave. Adam and Eve showed us how to lose our innocence. Jesus showed us how to get it back. He died in your place and conquered death for you! Now, everyone who trusts in Jesus as Savior and Lord is forgiven and made new in God's eyes.

Trusting in Jesus enables us to experience the thing we have been missing...*a right relationship with the living God!!!*

Still, the question remains, *"How can I know Jesus Christ as my Savior and Lord?"* Another great question!

In the book of Romans 10:9, the Bible says, *"...if you confess with your mouth the Lord Jesus and believe in your heart that God has raised Him from the dead, you will be saved."* This verse reveals the following requirements for knowing God:

- Believe that Jesus Christ truly is the virgin born Son of God.
- Believe that Jesus never sinned.
- Believe that Jesus Christ lived, died and rose from the grave in order to pay for your sins.
- Tell God that you want to live your life in away that honors Jesus Christ.

That is it! You become a brand new person with the Spirit of God living in you. You experience forgiveness, freedom, and joy. Not only that, *you become able to experience love the way God intended it.*

Perhaps today you have begun to realize that Jesus is who you have been searching for. Now you know exactly what you have been missing. Are you tired of spending your time in ways that leave you empty? *Don't you think it is time to begin a relationship with God?* If you are ready to know God personally, allow me to lead you in the following prayer:

DON'T YOU THINK IT IS TIME TO BEGIN A RELATIONSHIP WITH GOD?

> *"Dear God. I understand that I am a sinner. I realize that my sin has kept me from knowing you personally. I am so sorry that I have broken your heart with my sin. But God, I do believe that Jesus Christ is your Son. I believe that He lived a perfect life. I believe that He died and rose again to pay for MY sins. I am ready to live my life for you. Please forgive my sins and help me to know you personally."*

Although repeating my words cannot save you, God has forgiven you if you meant those words.

The book of I John 1:9 says, *"If we confess our sins, He is faithful and just to forgive us our sins and to cleanse us from all unrighteousness."*

If you prayed and meant those words, God has already begun to change you inside. You are forgiven. You are restored to your God. Now it is important that you get to know Him better. The following are some ways to do so:

- Get a Bible. Read it often.
- Talk to God often.
- Practice listening for His response.
- Get connected with a group of Christians (church) who meet weekly for Bible study.
- Look for those who live like they know God personally.

If you have trouble finding an encouraging church, contact our ministry. We will make a genuine effort to help you find a good church. You can contact us through our website at www.crosscultureministries.org.

ADDENDUM:

"WHAT IS COURTSHIP?"

"WHAT IS COURTSHIP?"

It seems as though most parents, young adults and teenagers today have grown up with the practice of dating. Throughout our lives, however, there has been the presence of an older generation. This generation has always spoken mysteriously of another time. During that time chivalry was expected of young men and courtship was the rule for young people who were interested in marriage. This generation of senior adults is a dying breed. Those who are concerned with negative effects of modern day romance on teenagers will do well to understand these senior adults and to explore the history behind this concept of courtship.

In the early days of our country, Puritans introduced the concept of courtship.[1] Although this concept has been revisited among the Christian culture recently, it has remained dormant among mainstream United States citizens for two generations. Therefore, it is necessary to understand the origin of courtship and how it differs from modern day dating among teenagers.

Puritans were opposed to non-marital sex and single-hood was viewed suspiciously. When a young man desired to court, he would receive permission from the father of the woman he was interested in.[2] This simple act of submission surely was deterrent to the possibility of pre-marital sex. The simple recognition that a girl belonged to her father above any "caller" suggests accountability. The tradition of actually talking personally to the father to receive permission would also serve the same purpose.

Perhaps much of the promiscuity in today's culture could be eliminated if boys were once again expected to meet the father of their date before taking her away from her home. When a boy is permitted to pull up in front of a young lady's house and blow the car horn to summon her away from her home, the action suggests that she is not worthy of much extra effort on the young man's part. When the girl can leave home without the young man coming into her father's house and recognizing that father as the authority and protector in her life, this also suggests that the boy in the driveway has more authority in her life than her own father. At such a point, God's primary plan of purity protection has been undermined and the girl's chances of returning home a virgin have greatly decreased. At least that is what the high rates of teen pregnancy, STD's and promiscuity seem to bear witness to.

From the mid 1800's until around 1920, courtship remained very formal. The man would request to visit the young woman in her home. Partners going off together to private places was frowned upon, and parents kept a close eye on the couple until the relationship was close to marriage.[3] In early America, the semblance of dating began with engagement. Couples rarely married if the parents did not approve. It was hoped that love would develop over time.[4] What a contradiction to modern dating! It is the common expectation today that dating is accompanied by sex and may never result in marriage at all. For the most part, the only young people who courted outside of the home were those whose homes were not large enough to provide the necessary balance of privacy and chaperonage.[5]

Calling, or even just visiting, was not a practicable system for young people whose families lived crowded into one or two rooms. For even the more established or independent working-class girls, the parlor and the piano often simply didn't exist. A "good time" increasingly became identified with public places and commercial amusements, making young women whose wages would not even cover the necessities of life dependent on men's "treats."[6] Many more serious young women were taking advantage of opportunities to enter the public world—going to college, taking jobs, entering and creating new urban professions.

Women who belonged to the public world by day began to demand fuller access to the public world in general. Though still considered risqué by some, dining out alone with a man or attending the theatre with no chaperone did not threaten an unmarried woman's reputation by the start of the twentieth century.[7] By 1920, the concept of dating had become popular. Popular "dates" were going to dances, movies, and out to eat. The automobile made dating more mobile and private, contributing to a rise in sexual activity.[8] The freedom that automobiles created for promiscuity has been portrayed on 50's television shows such as "Happy Days" where "necking" and "making out" were spun as something normal and desirable for teenagers who were dating. The women's movement and birth control also contributed to more permissive premarital sex and sex became common for people who were dating steady.[9]

There was more of a focus on romantic love as the basis for marriage. The media promoted sex. By 1937, the goal of dating among college students had shifted from love and mate selection to competition and pleasure.[10]

During the 1930's and 40's there was a rise in "steady" dating and the age of marriage reached an all time low for the 20th century, with the average being age 20 for women and 22 for men.[11] It is likely that this lowering of age was produced by the idea of romantic love. Such a concept as the primary prerequisite for marriage would certainly influence young people to marry the first person they felt emotionally and physically infatuated with.

In today's culture, people are marrying at much older ages. The average age of marriage in 2001 was 25 for women and 27 for men.[12] This is most likely because of the immaturity of today's generation. Young people are not expected to become self-supporting and are encouraged to take their time finding their way to happiness. The prolonging of marriage combined with the immaturity and promotion of sexual promiscuity is a recipe for disaster.

Today, young people, who are burning with passion in the prime of their sex drives, must decide if it is worth it to wait another 6 or 7 years for sexual intimacy. Many decide the wait is not worthwhile.

The historical digression from courtship to modern dating, combined with this burning passion has turned the healthy romance of our grandparents into a form of glorified prostitution. Many teenage boys and some teenage girls today sincerely believe that it is okay for a boy to expect sex from a date if he has spent a certain amount of money on her. Although teenagers must face such pressure in high schools, even greater challenges await them on college campuses. The young men in college act as if any woman is equally good; they are given not to falling in love with one, but to scoring in bed with many. And in this sporting attitude, they are now matched by some female trophy hunters.[13] Never mind wooing, today's collegians do not even make dates or other forward-looking commitments to see one another. In this, and in so many other ways, they reveal their blindness to the meaning of the passing of time. Those very few who couple off seriously and get married upon graduation as their parents once did are looked upon as freaks.[14]

Today's method of dating has also produced a lying heart among the romantic. The term "player" has become a popular term for someone who knows how to charm a member of the opposite sex, making him/her feel loved and using this to acquire sex from others. Many Americans are willing to present distorted images of themselves to increase the likelihood of getting dates. Men exaggerate sincerity, commitment, and income. Women are also willing to use many deceptions to enhance their physical appearance.[15]

The cheapening of sex through dating has also contributed to a rise in sexual crime. It is not surprising that a casual attitude toward sex would eventually lead to a casual attitude toward the body. In turn, the body becomes an object, rather than the vessel of a human being with emotions. A survey done in 1985 found that 25 percent of female respondents (age 17-19) reported experiencing forced sexual contact. This and other data suggests that adolescent date rape occurs and that even high school dating has a dark side characterized by coercion and sexual violence at an early age.[16]

Another way of thinking that has contributed to unhealthy dating practices is the idea that love is a feeling of the heart to be followed with reckless abandon. In earlier generations, strong feelings were not the only criteria for marriage. A level of maturity and dependability was expected of both partners. Currently, in the U.S, the idea of free, romantic love is promoted by the media and many young people have the misconception; that love allows them to "live happily ever after," to experience "love at first sight," and that "love overcomes all differences."[17] According to Stephanie Covington's book, *Leaving the Enchanted Forest:*

> "Obsessions, compulsions, and the temporary high of being 'in love' are neither love nor proof of

love; on the contrary, they are the signposts of falling in love-that tempting ecstatic feeling that can so easily lead to dependence and addiction." [18]

The decline in healthy romance has been steady and subtle. As times have changed, a generation has slowly become desensitized to what is proper in relating to the opposite sex. There also seems to be a loss of understanding as to what the purpose of marriage is. Finally, the definition of sex has become blurred to the point that casual acts of foreplay are not considered sex at all. The United States of America has finally produced a generation of teenagers who, as a unit, do not know God or understand His ways. These teenagers are not aware that much of their behavior toward the opposite sex is inappropriate, immoral, and destructive. Young people naturally believe that the world into which they were born is *the* world, the way the world not only is, but had to be, and they have no idea that they might be living in what is really act four or five of a tragedy. [19]

Turning a generation who has never known God, or a truly Christian society, back to truth and purity is a task too large for man. It is a God-sized task that only His word and Spirit can produce. The hope for teenagers today is in God's word. We must seek ways to infiltrate their culture, build trust and teach them to think biblically. Within this context, it will be helpful for parents to familiarize themselves with the concept of courtship. The difference between courtship and dating primarily is the intentions of the two involved and secondarily in the methods they employ. The intent of courtship is to pursue a relationship beyond acquaintance and toward engagement. Courtship generally facilitates purity and longevity. Dating is primarily centered around selfish desires for security and physical intimacy. Dating generally facilitates promiscuity and short relationships.

It is helpful to distinguish between undefined and directionless romances and a romantic relationship that is purposefully headed towards marriage.[20] In his book, "Boy Meets Girl," Joshua Harris provides sound teaching on the concept of courtship. Prior to the popularity of the book, an attempt was being made to return teenagers to sexual purity through the "True Love Waits" movement. For a while, however, such endeavors were falling short. Teenagers were signing pledge cards to wait until marriage before having sex. Although this is not a bad thing, the focus was still on sex rather than on worshipping God. Because of the vague understanding of what sex really is, teenagers understood their commitment as a promise to abstain from intercourse while continuing to explore foreplay. As a result, they were still consumed with sex and often were not able to fulfill their promise to abstain from intercourse.

Courtship removes focus from the physical altogether and encourages teenagers to move as far away from the line of sexual immorality as possible, rather than seeing how close they can get without having intercourse. Apparently, "True Love Waits" has recognized the above mindset and enhanced their program.

The time is fertile for teaching youth the concept of courtship. Teenagers have seen, firsthand, the results of the free-love movement of the 1960's and 70's. They have lived in the homes of an inconsistent generation of parents. They have felt the pain of divorce. It is high time that parents and leaders repent of our rebellion against tradition, confess this sin to God and our children, and get busy learning and teaching them a better way of romance. No longer can our nation afford to leave our children unchaperoned. No longer can we afford to allow some boy we don't know to take our daughter out when he has not bothered to meet us and ask our permission to do so. No longer can we afford to allow our daughters to dress provocatively. No longer can we afford to give our children material possessions as a replacement for our time and instruction in preparing them to be husbands and wives who glorify God!

In the Bible, Judges 2:7-10 speaks of a time when an older generation died out and the remaining generation of young people had been allowed to indulge in the ways of the culture around them. This young generation did not know the Lord, or the work which He had done for Israel. Later this generation experienced the judgment of God as they lost their freedom. The United States is currently losing the last generation who grew up knowing the benefits of courtship, among other truths.

A new generation is arising. This generation does not know the Lord or the things He has done for America. Never, in the past has God allowed a nation that once professed Him as Lord to turn away from righteousness without experiencing judgment. If we do not reach today's teenagers with truth, America's best days are over and surely judgment will follow.

The family is God's primary institution for teaching right from wrong. Courtship and dating are two extreme ways to prepare teenagers for marriage. The future blessings of our country could very well depend on a return to courtship! The challenge will be to re-introduce the concept of courtship within the modern culture. Although we must not be of the world in our thoughts and actions, Jesus prayed for God to protect us from evil as we remain in this world (John 17). We must begin now to pray for wisdom in seeking how to infiltrate this world once again with courtship for the Lord's sake.

BIBLIOGRAPHY:

Covington, Stephanie and Liana Beckett. *Leaving the Enchanted Forest (The Path From Relationship Addiction to Intimacy*. Harper & Row Publishers, San Francisco, c1988, pp. 158.

Hamon, Raeann R. and Bron B. Ingoldsby. *Mate Selection Across Cultures*. Sage publications, London, c2003, pp. 266.

Harris, Joshua. *Boy Meets Girl (Say Hello to Courtship)*. Multnomah Publishers, Sisters, Oregon, c2000, pp. 227.

Kass, Amy A. and Leon R. Kass. Wing to Wing, *Oar to Oar (Readings on Courting and Marrying)*. University of Notre Dame Press, Notre Dame, Indiana, c2000, pp. 630.

Pirog-Good, Maureen and Jan E. Stets. Violence in Dating Relationships (Emerging Social Issues. Praeger, New York, c1989, pp. 268.

NOTES:

[1]Hamon, Raeann R. and Bron B. Ingoldsby. *Mate Selection Across Cultures*. Sage Publications, London, c2003, p. 5

[2]Ibid, p. 5

[3]Ibid, p.7.

[4]Ibid, DO. 5-6.

[5]Ibid, p.7.

[6]Kass, Amy A. and Leon R. Kass. *Wing to Wing, Oar to Oar (Readings on Courting and Marrying)*. University of Notre Dame Press, Notre Dame, Indiana, c2000, p. 31.

[7]Ibid, p. 32.

[8]Hamon, Raeann R. and Bron B. Ingoldsby. *Mate Selection Across Cultures*. Sage Publications, London, c2003, p.7.

[9]Ibid, p.8.

[10]Ibid, p.7.

[11] Ibid, pp. 7-8.

[12]Kass, Amy A. and Leon R. Kass. *Wing to Wing, Oar to Oar (Readings on Courting*. University of Notre Dame Press, Notre Dame, Indiana, c2000, p.24.

[13]Ibid, p. 24.

[14]Hamon, Raeann R. and Bron B. Ingoldsby. *Mate Selection Across Cultures*. Sage Publications, London, c2003, p. 10.

[15]Pirog-Good, Maureen and Jan E. Stets. *Violence in Dating Relationships (Emerging Social Issues)*. Praeger, New York, c1989, p. 171.

[16]Hamon, Raeann R. and Bron B. Ingoldsby. *Mate Selection Across Cultures*. Sage Publications, London, c2003, pp. 12-13.

[17]Covington, Stephanie and Liana Beckett. *Leaving the Enchanted Forest (The Path From Relationship Addiction to Intimacy*. Harper & Row Publishers, San Francisco, c1988, p. 4.

[18] Ibid, p.4.

[19]Kass, Amy A. and Leon R. Kass. *Wing to Wing, Oar to Oar (Readings on Courting and Marrying)*. University of Notre Dame Press, Notre Dame, Indiana, c2000, p. 25.
[20]Harris, Joshua. *Boy Meets Girl (Say Hello to Courtship)*. Multnomah Publishers, Sisters, Oregon, c2000, p. 31.

ACKNOWLEDGMENTS

Several people have contributed to the production of this project. I would like to offer my sincere gratitude to the following persons:

God, my Father, for creating me with specific talents.

Jesus Christ, my Lord, for making it possible to serve in Your Kingdom.

Holy Spirit, for illuminating truth and equipping me to proclaim it.

My wife, Brantlee, for undying faithfulness and tireless efforts to listen, support, and offer feedback into my various ministry quests. Thank you sooooo...much for being my number one encourager and accountability partner in life. I love you.

My children, Caleb, Drew, Hannah & Hope for embracing this ministry life and loving me in spite of my shortcomings as a Dad. You have been troopers all these years of burning up the highways, sleeping in all kinds of places, and living an "out of the box" life. You are each amazing and unique. I love watching you grow up in Christ! Without your willingness to adapt, I would not have time to work on projects like One Love.

My mentor and friend, Pastor Dan Jividen, for always being a "straight shooter" in my life. Thanks for taking time to proof-read, edit and provide an honest "take" on this book.

Matt Evans, I am thankful for the many times and ways God has allowed us to serve together over the years. Your work ethic is off the chart. God has given you a wonderful talent for songwriting. He has gifted you with compassion as a counselor while anointing you to lead believers in worship. BUT WAIT, He has also given you a rare ability to connect with unsaved audiences through music. I am blessed every time we minister together. Thanks for writing the songs and overseeing the production of the ONE LOVE music c.d.

Brooke Horn for the many hours you have spent on this project. You are a great project manager. Thank you for ALL you have contributed from design and layout, to photography and graphics, to editing, to being the chief PR person for the book and c.d. I am so impressed with the level of excellence with which you represent Jesus in all you do. You are a great servant of God. May He richly reward and bless you through this project.

Wayne Church for your help in setting up our website and tending to various web-related needs. You have always accepted opportunities to serve through CCM with joy and enthusiasm. I am so glad I know some of your testimony. God has brought you through some unique trials and His light shines through you. Stay the course.

Jim Everhart, for donating your time to keep our finances in order. You are a true answer to prayer. God has definitely given CCM a top notch financial manager who helps keep this ministry above reproach. May your joy be full as you continue to steward your gifts for His glory.

CCM's board of Directors (Daniel Rice, Jim Rice, Marcus Howard, Steve King), your continual commitment to keep this ministry accountable and offer encouragement is such a blessing to this evangelist. I am honored to submit to your authority. Thanks for supporting this project with enthusiasm.

Todd and Sharon Shoe for continually supporting CCM in various ways. Thanks especially for the different ways you have contributed to this specific project. CCM and I are honored to have an advocate of your quality. You demonstrate assertiveness, discipline, and excellence in all that you undertake. Most of all, you honor God with the blessings He has bestowed upon you. The Elwell family is thankful to call you our friends.

"The Green Family Charitable Foundation" and Jennifer Kent. Thank you for taking the time to review this project and for helping us get it done. May God continue to multiply His blessings through you for His Kingdom's sake.

Marty Dupree. Thank you, my dear brother, for taking time to read, pray, and write the foreword to One Love. You are such a tremendous soul winner. I love the compassion you demonstrate for our Lord, Jesus Christ, and those He came to save. You are a shining example of a righteous husband and father. You are a great servant, teacher, and friend of the local church. I'm sure my fellow evangelists will agree you are like a fountain of fresh water sent from God encouraging us to stay faithful to the call. At a time when our culture and many churches seem unsure what to do with an evangelist, God has placed you in the Kingdom as an advocate. I thank God upon every remembrance of you. To borrow from your own words, "Every blessing to you in the Lord Jesus Christ."

Dr. Daniel Akin, Dr. David Horton, Dr. Charles Whipple, Bruce Cannon, Taylor Field, Nate Garrett. The ONE LOVE Team and I are incredibly blessed and amazed that you took time to read and endorse this project. You each have huge responsibilities in God's Kingdom work. Time is so valuable. Thank you so very much for investing into this work.

Andy Cockrell and Darrin Cherry for hosting and advocating our ONE LOVE conferences.

Natalie Denning for taking the time to read the manuscript. Your feedback as a college student has been extremely encouraging to me.
Those whose testimonies are shared in this book, you know who you are and you know to Whom you belong. Your stories are the real life witness of the power of God's truth.

Crystal Faulkiner and Olivia Voltaggio. Thank you, Crystal for sharing your joy and capturing our 'good side.' And to Olivia for your sweet spirit that helped bring out our smiles.

BRING
ONE LOVE
CONFERENCES
TO YOUR
CHURCH
OR SCHOOL!

ONE LOVE:
EXTREME EXPERIENCE

A ministry of
Cross Culture Ministries
PO Box 4144
Greensboro, NC 27404
336.282.8500

Find us on Facebook:
ONE LOVE Book
Cross Culture Ministries

www.onelovebook.org
www.crosscultureministries.org

COLLIDE
MISSION CAMPS

>>LEWISBURG, WV

Join hands with local churches to provide service projects and children's day camps to connect with unreached people in their communities.

GREENSBORO, NC<<

Experience urban ministry by serving and leading day camps in partnership with Greensboro Boys & Girls Clubs.

>>JAMAICA

Share the love of Christ on an unforgettable journey as we partner with Jim Rice Ministries and local Jamaican churches in reaching their culture for Christ.

>>> FOR MORE INFO <<<

CROSS CULTURE MINISTRIES
www.crosscultureministries.com
336.282.8500

131